SWITZERLAND

AT THE BEGINNING OF THE SIXTEENTH CENTURY

5.00
10/01

JOHNS HOPKINS UNIVERSITY STUDIES

IN

HISTORICAL AND POLITICAL SCIENCE

(Edited by H. B. Adams, 1882-1901)

J. M. VINCENT

J. H. HOLLANDER   W. W. WILLOUGHBY

Editors

———

SWITZERLAND

AT THE BEGINNING OF THE SIXTEENTH CENTURY

BY

JOHN MARTIN VINCENT

———

AMS PRESS

NEW YORK

Reprinted from the edition of 1904, Baltimore
First AMS EDITION published 1971
Manufactured in the United States of America

International Standard Book Number: 0-404-06768-9

Library of Congress Number: 72-149671

AMS PRESS INC.
NEW YORK, N.Y. 10003

CONTENTS.

PREFATORY NOTE.

This study was originally written as an introduction to the biography of Zwingli by Professor Samuel Macauley Jackson, in his series of " Heroes of the Reformation." In the preparation more materials were collected than could be used in a chapter intended primarily for the general reader, consequently it seemed to be advisable to bring forward the subject again with additional citations of sources and with further indications of the problems involved.

The courtesy of the former editor and publishers is gratefully acknowledged.

SWITZERLAND AT THE BEGINNING OF THE SIXTEENTH CENTURY.

CHAPTER I.

POLITICAL CONDITIONS.

At the close of the fifteenth century the traveller in Switzerland would have found the prevailing races and languages firmly established in the places which they occupy to-day, but the people were not bound together by the same ties of government. Germans in the north and east, French in the west and south had long grown fast to the rocky soil, but they were grouped in small independent States, and lived under most diverse political conditions. For a long time there had existed a Swiss Confederation, but this did not include a considerable number of the present members. Yet it must be said that most of the territory now known as Switzerland was in some manner attached to it by friendly alliances and by ties of common interest, so that in relation to outside nations they all stood together. The distinguishing feature of the Confederation was, however, the feebleness of its unity within and the absolute independence of the separate States in matters of law and government. This fact had much to do with the history of the Reformation in Switzerland. So also had the previous history of some of the prominent States and cities.

The Swiss Confederation began in a union of three small German cantons in the centre of the country, all of them touching upon the Lake of Lucerne. At the outset this was a league of pastoral republics, whose wild and mountainous territory was not over thirty-five miles square. To this nucleus, however, were soon added neighbouring districts and cities, till, in the year 1353, they became the " League of Eight." For a century and a quarter this was the extent of the Confederation. Uri, Schwyz, Unterwalden, Zug, Glarus, Lucerne, Zurich, and Bern were the members of the Union during the heroic struggle for freedom from the German Empire. Although they enjoyed the friendly assistance of others, this was also the extent of the Confederation in the " glorious period " of the Burgundian wars, when Charles the Bold was defeated in 1476, and when, for a time, these mountaineers became the arbiters of Europe. Just at the opening of the sixteenth century the number of confederated cantons was increased to thirteen by the addition of Basel, Schaffhausen, and Appenzell, while States like Geneva, Neuchâtel, and the Grisons remained in the position of friendly allies.

Part of this Confederation consisted of rural democracies engaged in pastoral or agricultural pursuits and governing themselves with most complete democracy. The other members were flourishing city States, like Bern, Lucerne, Zurich, and Basel, whose municipal population followed commerce and industry with varying intensity, and whose governments were more or less aristocratic. The original mountain States enjoyed the proud distinction of having founded Swiss freedom, but by this time the leadership in State policy as well as in general civilisation lay with the cities. Among these Zurich and Bern were pre-eminent in political influence.

Toward the cities the rural cantons exhibited a jealousy which had for a long time prevented any additions to the Confederation and afterward caused trouble in federal politics. It was feared that the cities would endeavour to absorb the powers of the rural States, or, by their votes in the Diet, enact measures oppressive to the country people. This suspicion was not without some foundation, for the governments of the cities had been in the habit of treating the rural population of their own territories with less consideration. They often discriminated against the industry and productions of the people outside the walls of the towns and gave the city dwellers superior rights.

On the other hand, the city States were greater in population, wealth, and intelligence, but the great city of Bern had no more votes in the Confederation than the tiny democracy of Uri. Friction naturally followed, and occasionally there were open hostilities, followed by armed conflict. At times there were recriminations by means of duties on goods and by shutting off routes of transportation. On both sides great selfishness had been displayed, but the small cantons had been, on the whole, more obstinate, for they had, at times, nearly sacrificed the Confederation to maintain their local interests. Hence we may expect to find great contrasts between the actions of the various parts of Switzerland when new doctrines of religion upheave the established order of thinking.

The great arena of political action was the federal congress, called the Diet, which met at stated intervals in the various large cities alternately. This Diet was an assembly of delegates from the various cantons, who came together to deliberate and to pass resolutions on matters of common interest. The passing of resolutions and recommendations was in reality the limit of their legislative power, for the delegations could not vote finally without the consent of their home governments. No act could be passed without the unanimous consent of all the cantons, and when a law was enacted there was no central government to enforce it. The execution of the laws was left to the cantonal governments, and there was no one to punish infraction except the offenders themselves. Consequently federal laws were obeyed in those States which saw fit to enforce them.

Federal government, therefore, was a system of treaties and agreements chiefly touching foreign relations. The welfare of the citizen lay in the hands of his canton. To that he owed his allegiance and patriotic devotion, and from that he obtained protection in the enjoyment of his liberties. The history of the reformation in the Church revolves about the fact that each State determined for itself the form of worship in its own territory.   In spite of this independent sovereignty, however, the political destiny of the nation lay, in considerable measure, in the hands of the Diet, for agreements with foreign Powers were made by that assembly.[1]

---

[1] " In the year of our Lord, 1478, there was a great Diet at Zürich and to this Diet the king of France sent his excellent councillors. There came also Duke Reinhard, of Lorraine, in person with thirty horses.   There came also Duke Sigmund's excellent councillors, namely, Hildebrand Rasp, Marquart Von Schellenberg, kt., Antoine Geissberg, Hans Lantz and Hans Bruchle with forty horses.   There came also the Burgundians with many horses, also the excellent councillors of the Bishop and the City of Strasbourg and of the Bishop and City of Basel, likewise came also the delegates from Colmar and Schlettstadt.   Likewise all the delegates of the confederates who belong to the great League.   So also many honorable people, princes and lords of lands and cities who were useful to the Confederation sent their ambassadors hither so that it was a great diet such as had never been before within the memory of man. This same diet continued three weeks and began on Monday after the twelfth day in that same year (during this time), a fresh bird cost two shillings and something more and while all things were dear and not easy to get, a measure of wine grown in the same year was worth nine pounds in the keg, ¯yet the authorities began to make presents to the foreign visitors."   Edilbach's Chronicle.   Mittheilungen der Antiq. Ges., in Zürich, Bd. 4.

CHAPTER II.

MERCENARY SERVICE.

At the beginning of the sixteenth century the Swiss were much courted by foreign governments desiring mercenary soldiers, and foreign ambassadors were constantly appearing before the authorities with weighty requests. A meeting of the Diet in 1512 at the city of Baden may serve as an example. The minutes for August 11 inform us that on that day in the hall of assembly the deputy of the Duke of Lorraine read a message respecting the passage of soldiers through that province. A representative of the Pope presented to the Confederation a sword, a hat, and two banners, together with privileges contained in a Bull, as honourable rewards for faithful services. An embassy from the King of Spain requested that the Confederation should join in the league which had been formed between the Pope, the King of Spain, and the Republic of Venice. An embassy from the duke of Savoy hoped that former agreements with him would be maintained. Imperial ambassadors desired the confederates to join in a campaign in Burgundy. A motion was offered on the relations of the Confederation to the Duchy of Milan. An embassy from the Republic of Venice desired to negotiate a treaty with the Swiss, and received answer that the conflict between the Emperor and the Venetians must be smoothed over before the Diet could consider the matter. On the following day further hearings were given to these powers, and proposals were entertained which involved cessions of territory and large pecuniary rewards for military services.

Thus we may see that the Swiss at the turning of the century were not an obscure people, busied only with their own affairs. They formed for the moment a European Power,

whose good-will and services were sedulously courted. The
soldiers of Switzerland fought in the armies of all the great
States, sometimes on one side and sometimes on another, and
were even found in opposing camps. The effects of this
upon politics and morality were far reaching, for the Swiss
at this time were not fighting for independence, nor in self-
defence, but for the mercenary rewards of the employing
Powers.

The Diet was not the only authority brought in contact
with foreign monarchs. Its meeting was a convenient place
to negotiate with all Switzerland at once, but it was necessary to deal with the cantonal governments also. Every little
capital or legislature was approached by foreign emissaries
on the subject of military aid. Enlistment was carried on by
the States themselves, and contracts were made with foreign
governments for the services of the companies required. In-
duced by the high pay and opportunities for plunder, the
hardy mountaineers eagerly ventured into any war. The de-
moralizing effects of this system appeared not alone among
the soldiery and in private life. Official corruption was uni-
versal, and was taken so much as a matter of course that it
brought no disgrace to public men.

In order to gain favour with these statesmen, foreign monarchs vied with each other in granting subsidies, pensions
and special bribes. Persons in authority even accepted gifts
from two or more Powers at the same time, and voted for the
side which appeared the more profitable. Patriotism sank to
a very low ebb, and statesmanship was busier with its rewards than with its duties. Money flowed into the country
through numerous channels. There was the bounty to the
State itself for its contingent, then the pensions to the statesmen for granting the same, followed by the pay of the soldiers themselves, and such plunder as they might have cap-
tured or ransomed while away. When the size and number
of the mercenary contingents are taken into consideration,
it will be seen that a large proportion of the population was
in greater or less degree dependent on the foreign subsidies.
The effect of this was not slow in coming.

Even before the beginning of the sixteenth century the lawmakers, both cantonal and federal, had been conscious of the evil, and had been endeavouring to check enlistment in foreign service. The Diet repeatedly passed resolutions on the subject, but these were for the most part feeble attempts to prevent irregular and unofficial enlistments. For example, in 1479, it was resolved that every canton should require its soldiers to take oath not to go privately into foreign war. Some thought that offenders should be punished with death. The territorial governors were ordered to capture and imprison all soldiers who had been fighting under the German Emperor, and to hold them till they should pay five pounds fine and should take oath not to enlist without permission of the authorities. In 1488, the German Emperor, on his side, requested the confederates not to allow their soldiers to enlist in France without permission. The Governor of Baden was ordered to punish soldiers returning from France with ten pounds fine or imprisonment. In 1492, another ordinance against unauthorized enlistment recommended a fine with imprisonment on bread and water.[1]

From time to time complaints were brought against the catonal governments because they did not suppress " running away to war," and, on the other hand, cantons asked aid of the confederates to suppress the evil. Yet the anxiety seems to have been caused more by the irregularities than by the mercenary system itself. In 1498, a petition was received from Swiss soldiers serving against France in the armies in Burgundy requesting that no contingents from the Confederation be allowed to fight against them. The same Diet received an embassy from the Emperor of Germany with a mission to disentangle other complications arising from simultaneous enlistment in the service of that country.[2]

---

[1] The acts of the Diet are to be found in the *Amtliche Sammlung der Eidgenössischen Abschiede*, 1245-1798, in 8 vols., 4to, published by the Swiss Federal Government. These documents are not exactly minutes of the Diet, but instructions given to the delegates at the adjournment of each meeting as to what they should refer to their home governments. Citations may be traced by the dates.

[2] See Appendix I.

The root of the evil was discovered in due time, but it was difficult to work any reform, for the lawmakers themselves were entangled.   The acceptance of pensions from foreign governments was common among the statesmen of all countries at this time.   Public sentiment did not appear to frown on the practice unless in flagrant cases of disloyalty.   Hence it is not surprising that the evil consequences were not immediately condemned in Switzerland.   Furthermore, the military profession was a welcome career to the hard-worked peasantry of every canton, and offered rich and rapid rewards in place of the slow returns of ordinary labour.

The time came, however, when good citizens, observing the moral effect of these things, endeavoured not only to regulate enlistment but to suppress the pension system entirely.   Resolutions, offered from time to time, condemned the practice and urged the States to prohibit the entrance of pension money into their borders.   A notable example of this was an agreement brought forward in the Diet of July, 1503.   The cantons were asked to enforce a law to this effect:

" That no one in the Confederation, whether he be townsman, countryman, or subject peasant, clerical or layman, noble or unnoble, rich or poor, of whatever rank or condition, shall from this day on receive from emperors, kings, princes, lords, or cities, spiritual or temporal powers, or from anyone whomsoever, any pension, service money, provision, allowance, salary, or gifts, whether this come to himself or through his wife, children, servants, or others, whereby it come to his use, either secretly or openly."

Any person who shall be convicted of disobedience to this order shall be

" forever removed from the honours and offices which he may have, and shall not be employed in honourable affairs, as in courts of justice, councils, embassies, and such matters, but from that hour on he shall be arrested by the proper authorities and punished in person and goods as they may think best."

Although this resolution was accepted by all the cantons, it was not an easy matter to enforce, for the enlistment itself was not stopped. According to the same act, recruiting must be official, and only irregular running away to war was to be punished. The pensions went on as before, and in a few years the law was abrogated by a resolution to allow the cantons to do as they pleased.[4]

In the Italian campaigns of the first two decades of the sixteenth century the Swiss suffered severe losses in men, but the effect of this was to bring more money into the country, for soldiers were harder to obtain. In consequence of the treaties entered into between 1516 and 1521 Switzerland was deluged with coin. From France there were annual subsidies of 3000 livres to each of the cantons, and to the Confederation as a whole a sum of 700,000 crowns was offered in one payment as indemnity for the wars of 1513 and 1515. At the same time the Duke of Milan agreed to pay 150,000 ducats at once and 40,000 ducats annually. Besides these sums there were subsidies from Austria and from the Pope. Although these promises were not always punctually fulfilled, nevertheless a constant stream of foreign gold poured into the valleys of Helvetia.[5]

---

[4] 1508, July 4. Eidg. Abschiede III, pt. 2, pp. 383, 385, 424, 425, 427, 430.

[5] The sums above mentioned have a present silver value of about $1,871,600, but the purchase power was many times greater at the beginning of the sixteenth century. See Hilty, Les Constitutions Fédérales de la Suisse, 183 sq.

CHAPTER III.

The opinions of certain foreign observers of the time are not flattering. For instance, Balcus, an ambassador from Milan, wrote between the years 1500 and 1504 a description of the Confederation, in which the annoyances of a foreigner are mingled with valuable impressions of the people. Coming from the bright skies of Italy and from the higher civilisation of the southern cities, it is not to be expected that the Italians would be altogether pleased with their mountain neighbours.

Says Balcus:

" Although the Swiss are altogether unhewn barbarians, yet they live among themselves according to certain laws which they consider so holy that no one dare to break or overstep them, because it is a crime to have broken them even in the slightest. Our civil law, however, our good manners and honourable customs, and, what is worse, their own laws and ordinances respecting other nations, they do not themselves observe at all, because they are without fidelity, uprightness, and humanity; but they seize rudely everything before them, building upon obstinacy, not upon wisdom."

" When they start out to war they swear a solemn oath that every man who sees one of his comrades desert, or act the coward in battle, will cut him down on the spot, for they believe that the courage and persistency of warriors is greater when they, out of fear of death, do not fear death."

" In peace, however, and when one citizen brings complaints against another citizen, they bind themselves also by

---

⁶ Balcus, Descriptio Helvetiæ, edited by Bernouilli for Quellen zur Schweizergeschichte, vi., 78. Oechsli, Quellenbuch, ii., 470.

an oath, for, if they have any business with one another and
fall into strife, as it often happens, and seize their weapons
or begin to curse each other, if then another party comes
forward, places himself in their midst, and begs them to lay
down the weapons and to talk over the matter in peace, and
commands them to be peaceful, and if one of the contending
parties will not hearken, the man who offers himself as a
peacemaker is bound by oath to kill him, and that without
punishment."

" They begin a battle after they have formed their phalanx
according to the old methods of war, and steadfast and fear-
less, they are almost indifferent to life and death. In court
they judge not according to the written laws but according
to common custom, and believe that nothing is more favourable to justice than a quick judgment, wherefore they over-
throw the procedures and sentences of court. To curse God
and heavenly things is regarded by them as a crime worthy of
death, and if any one of them is prosecuted they do not allow
any pity to prevent him from being punished according to
the law."

" Although accustomed to robbery yet the people have an
extravagant generosity to the poor. The scholars in the
study of Latin, if there are any such, beg their living with
singing. Their stately but remarkably extravagant daily
meals they spin out to great length, so that they spend two
to three hours at table eating their many dishes and barbar-
ous spices with much noise and conversation. They show
ill-will against those who despise this kind of table pleasure."

" When princely ambassadors arrive, the heads of the city,
or certain ones from the council visit them immediately to
give them greeting. At breakfast or supper there is a con-
tinual crowd around them, including not only the invited or
important persons in office, but with these many insignificant
people. All these the ambassadors must receive in a friendly
way and feed them richly, otherwise they will be followed
with perpetual hate and ill-will. In among these will creep
also clowns and jugglers and whoever understands amusing

arts, and one must receive this kind of people, admire their
wit, and before going away must leave them some kind of a
present or reward for their art.   Furthermore the council is
accustomed to send to every ambassador, daily, several measures of wine at the hours for breakfast and supper.   The
persons who bring these things are rewarded by the re-
ceiver of the gift with a small goldpiece, and at his departure
with at least one more goldpiece.   Whereupon the whole
expense is charged to public good and advantage."

" Custom allows that women, who on account of the beauty
of their faces and the attraction of their persons are uncom-
monly lovable, may be embraced and kissed anywhere and by
anybody without distinction.[7]   The cultivation of the intellect is rare and the noble virtues receive no honour.   This
low-born people, this lot of peasants, born in mountains and
woods and brought up in a narrow hole, have begun to play
the lord in Europe, and think nothing of enlarging the borders of their own dominion if anyone allows them the opportunity to do so. Moreover, there is no doubt that wars, peace,
the victories and the misfortunes of famous kings, depend
upon them.   This little band of cowherds and shepherds,
who pass the day in the drawing and the thickening of milk ;
who are, so to speak, without law and ignorant of things
human and divine; will prescribe laws for all others and sit
in judgment on the affairs of princes, as though the appeal
and the highest judgment belonged to them.   For assumption and violent passion, the diseases which are so near to
madness, they surpass all other mortal beings, but among
themselves they agree so well together that as a reward and
fruit of their unity they enjoy an undisturbed and contin-
uous freedom, to which indeed the quarrels of others have
given assistance."

Johannes Trithemius, a learned German abbot, writing of
the wars of the Swabian League, included the following
description of the Swiss.[8]

---

[7] Erasmus says this was true in England at the time (Letter to
Anderlin, Epis., lxv., quoted by Froude, Life and Letters, p. 45.)
[8] Annales Hirsaugienses, ii., 572 (Edit. 1690) ; Oechsli, Quellenbuch, i., 282.

" Whether the Confederates have had a just or an unjust cause for war is not for me to decide, since I do not hold the place of a judge. But this I say, this I write and hand on in writing to the future world, which everybody knows to-day who has lived with us in Germany, and which all say, who know the manner of the Swiss, that they are a people proud by nature, enemies of princes, riotous, and for a long time have been contrary and disobedient to their overlords; filled with contempt for others and full of assumption for themselves; deceitful in war and lovers of treason; in peace never steadfast; nor do they inquire about the justice of what is due from them by law, especially when it affects the independence which they have the effrontery to assume. I say nevertheless that they are not only bold in war but also shrewd, and they are mutually helpful in time of need, and no one leaves another in danger, nor do the rich despise the poor."

In 1504, Jacob Wimpheling, one of the literary lights of the period, presented to the Elector of Mainz a remarkable address in the form of a prayer for the conversion of the Swiss. He takes advantage of his position before the Throne to bring in a scathing indictment of that people. Among other things he says:

" In the capture of prisoners there is more humanity to be found among Turks and Bohemians than among the Swiss."

" Their laws and ordinances when summed up are three: We will not; we will; you must."

" Pope Pius II, in agreement with us, complains greatly of this. He says that they are a proud people by nature who will not act according to justice, unless this justice is serviceable to them, and they hold nothing for right except when it agrees with their fantastic ideas. And how can they truly understand right and justice, when their lives are spent, not in the study of the philosophers nor of the laws of the Emperor, but in arms and warfare?"[9]

---

[9] Oechsli, Quellenbuch, I., 282. Soliloqium Wimphelingi.

The German Humanist, Pirckheimer, in his contemporary history of a war in which the Swiss had been engaged, characterises the military prowess of that people.[10] After a description of the Burgundian campaign he continues as follows:

" In the meanwhile the Swiss rested from the alarms of war, for no power was so great after the suppression of the Burgundians that it would have dared to challenge them. They permitted forces to be sent now to Maximilian, now to the French not only because they wished to exercise their youth in warlike discipline, but also because they feared, or rather, hated both, and the success of either party roused their anger. In truth, all Germans have received from the Swiss the weapons and the military tactics which they now use, for they threw away the shield which they had formerly been accustomed to use, like all other nations. They learned through experience that the shield could not in any way withstand the power of the phalanx and of the lance· Therefore, up to my time, all those who carried spears, halberds, and swords, were called Swiss, even if they were born in the middle of Germany, until finally, on account of hatred of the Swiss, the name ' Landsknecht,' that is, soldiers from the home country, came up and began to be famous."

Macchiavelli [11] makes frequent references to the military reputation of the Swiss and to the resulting political independence. He is more or less indifferent to the moral effects of these facts.

" From experience one observes armed republics making the greatest progress, but mercenary armies bring on nothing but evil ; and it is more difficult for a republic to fall into the power of one of its citizens, when it is armed with its own weapons than when it is armed with foreign weapons. Rome and Sparta remained many centuries armed and free. The Swiss are the most thoroughly armed and the freest of nations."

---

[10] Pirckheimer, Hist. belli Suitensis, p. 11 ; Oechsli, Quellenbuch, i., 285.
[11] The Prince, chap. xii.

He also speaks of the Swiss as " the teachers of the modern art of war," whose formations and tactics " every nation has imitated."

Guicciardini, in his History of Italy,[12] is obliged to touch upon its relations with Switzerland. He gives a calm review of the institutions of the country, but the effects of the mercenary service on moral character are plainly discernible.

" The Swiss are of the same kind as those who are called Helvetians by the ancients, and a race which dwells in mountains higher than the Jura. . . . They are divided into thirteen peoples (they call them cantons), each one of which rules itself with its own magistrates, laws, and ordinances. They order every year or oftener, as occasion arises, a discussion of their common affairs, assembling at this or that place, as the delegates of the cantons decide. They call these assemblies, according to German usage, Federal Diets, at which they decide upon war, peace, or treaties, or consider the requests of those who demand soldiers or volunteers, and all other things which concern their common interests. When the cantons grant mercenaries by law, they themselves choose a captain to whom the army, with the flag, is entrusted in the name of the State. This terrible and unlearned people have made a great name for unity and skill in arms, with which, by their natural bravery and the discipline of their tactics, they have not only powerfully defended their own country, but also outside of their native land they have exercised the arts of war with the greatest reputation. But this would have been immeasurably greater if they had used it for their own authority, not for pay and the extension of the dominion of others, or if they had had before their eyes nobler aims than the lust for money. From love of this they lost the opportunity to make all Italy fruitful, for, since they came from home only as hired soldiers, they have carried away for their State no fruits of their victories. . . . At home the important people are not ashamed to take presents and pensions from foreign princes, as inducements to

---

[12] Guicciardini, La Historia d'Italia, Book X., cap. iii., anno 1511.

take their side and favour them in the councils. As by this means they have mixed their private interests with public affairs, and have become purchasable and bribe-takers, so disunion has crept in among them. After the practice had once begun that those things which had been agreed to by the majority of the cantons at the Diet, were not followed by all the States, they finally came a few years ago into open war with each other, from which followed the greatest injury to the reputation which they had everywhere enjoyed."

The comments of these more or less unsympathetic foreigners are confirmed by the observations of native writers, like the Humanist, Bonifacius Amerbach of Basel: " If there ever was a time, the word of the poet is now true, ' this is, indeed, the age of gold.' " [13]

---

[13] Letter to Zasius, 1520. Burckhardt, B. Amerbach und die Reformation, p. 138. De novis quid scribam ignoro, adeo cottidie nova subinde rerum est facies. Si unquam, nunc maxime apud nos verum est poëtae illud: aurea sunt vere nunc saecula. Legati principum et Regum frequentes apud nos sunt. Rex Francorum tinnulis suis rationibus nos (sic) tantum non persuasit, et iam de foedere ineundo cogitamus. Praeter enim solita et ea satis ampla cum privatis tum reip. Helveticae pensa stipendia, promittit nunc cuilibet per totam Helvetiam senatori annuatim coronatos XX, ad haec sextumviris et iis qui ad comitia, ut ita nominem, curiata convocari solent, singulis annis X. Denique nihil non parat ad irretiendos horum animos. Non amplius aureorum quondam temporum recordamur, cum nunc toti aurei simus. Quid inde futurum sit, pronunciare nec si volo possum nec si possum volo. Vereor tamen, ne idem nobis contingat quod olim Spartanis oraculo proditum est: una fames auri Spartam capiet subigetque, praeterea nihil.

CHAPTER IV.

MORALITY OF THE PEOPLE.

The effect of the military service was brutalising. The foreign gold so easily obtained brought with it corruption of morals. The chronicler Anshelm of Bern, writing about the year 1500, complains bitterly of the changes seen in the manners and customs of the people. To be sure, he excites himself over many unessential matters of dress, but they all indicate to him a passion for extravagance and luxury leading to moral debasement. Such were shaggy hats with many ostrich plumes for men, cloth from London and Lombardy, long coats with many folds, silk jackets even for peasants, parti-coloured stockings, slashed shoes with rings on the toes, silver pipes and silk sashes. To his mind all these go with gambling, disorderly shouting, extravagant dances, over-much eating, and the consumption of foreign wines, confections and spices. Rich men built themselves great houses with high glass windows full of painted coats of arms. Women, likewise, must have costly dresses and ornaments, " and as these expensive manners have increased, so in the same measure have increased the lust for honours and goods, trickery and unfaithfulness, unbelief, haughtiness, pride, debauchery, scorn, and with them all arts for gaining money, especially those things which serve the tongue [palate] and trades which are serviceable to luxurious pride." [14]

As we have noted in other connections, magistrates and authorities were to some extent aware of the evils of the time and endeavoured to stop the progress of corruption. It would be unfair to measure their efforts by standards of the

---

[14] Anshelm, Berner-Chronik (Anno, 1503). Oechsli, Quellenbuch, ii., 464.

nineteenth century, but we can see that the lawmakers only trimmed the twigs of the tree so long as they failed to prohibit foreign pensions. They tried to stop the descent of moral character by laws against luxury and new fashions. Their intentions were excellent, but their efforts apparently unavailing. It is a wide-spread belief that " blue-laws " were an invention of the Puritans, but in reality they began in antiquity and continued through the Middle Ages into modern times. Sumptuary ordinances were repeatedly enacted in the cities of Switzerland before the Reformation, and a few may be cited here to show how they attempted to regulate private conduct in those days.

In Basel, in 1441-42, it was forbidden to play dice in the guilds, or club-houses. Betting must on no account exceed four or five pence. After the nine o'clock bell the house master and servants should stop all playing and send the guests home, in order that profane swearing and cursing might be prevented. Wedding feasts which often took place at the guild-house, were limited to one day and to a fixed expenditure.

Likewise at Zurich, in the ordinances of 1488, we read that " No citizen shall in future extend his wedding feast over more than one day." If he is a member of an aristocratic guild, and consequently able to bear the expense, he may invite the ladies of the guild, otherwise no one except the relatives may come. It seems to have been the custom to give presents to the guests. A maximum of five shillings is fixed for this for each person, while bride and groom receive no gifts whatever. Extravagance at christenings is to be stopped by fixing the limit of gifts, and other festivals in like manner.

The effect of the influx of foreign money and foreign fashions seems to have been felt in 1488. The Zurich ordinance on the subject reads as follows:

" In view of the marked disorder which has begun in our city among the common people on account of the costly clothing which their wives and daughters wear, and in order to prevent this, we have ordained that hereafter no woman or girl shall in any wise wear silver- or gold-plated pins, rings, or buckles, nor any silk garment or trimming on coats, shoes, neckwear, etc., except the women of the guilds of the *Rüden* and *Schnecken.* Further, no woman of the community shall have a mounted girdle, except those whose husbands possess 1000 gulden or over, and they may have one such girdle and no more to the value of about 12 gulden. These persons may also have silk borders and trimmings on their bodices with modesty, but without hooks and buckles as above said. If anyone acts contrary to this, such forbidden girdles shall be confiscated to the city, and whoever already has such girdles, whether few or many, shall sell the same, or allow their husbands to sell them for his business and necessities. As to buckles, rings, and silk, everyone who disobeys this ordinance shall pay two marks of silver for each offence." [15]

The federal government of Switzerland also occupied itself with sumptuary laws from time to time and seemed particularly incensed at the new fashioned men's jackets. The following are examples from the latter part of the 15th century.[16]

" 1481, 19th March. Is the opinion of the delegates that laws ought to be established everywhere in the confederation against the shameful short clothing. That no one should have their clothes made so short that they do not cover their shame before and behind. As often as any one shall put on a shorter garment he shall be fined one gulden. A tailor that makes such clothes shall be fined two gulden."

" 1484, 14th January. In regard to short shameful clothes which are a scandal before God and the world, also to the long daggers and swords which the soldiers carry either half or wholly unsheathed, concerning the wicked oaths, the extravagant life and dangerous actions, also concerning the

---

[15] Reprinted in Oechsli, i., 209. See Vincent, " European Blue Laws," Report Am. Hist. Assoc., 1897, pp. 357-372; cf. p. 361 sqq.
[16] Eidgenösaische Abschiede.

irregular enlisting and going away to war each canton ought to establish it's own ordinances and out of these a special ordinance for the confederation should be made at the next assembly."

" 1492, 28th of June. Every delegate knows what to report in regard to the pleasure of the assembly respecting extravagant clothing and daggers, and the wearing of swords in half sheathes."

" 1492, 11, August. Respecting improper clothing the people of Schwyz have ordained that under penalty no one shall wear clothing except such as covers their shame before and behind and shall not wear more than one, two or three colors. Every delegate shall report this fact in order that the other cantons can make the same ordinances."

Such were the paternal efforts of the lawmakers of the end of that century. Their enactments are amusing to read and were ineffectual at the time, but they show the direction of popular tendencies. This ordinance of Zurich was, indeed, the work of a dictator, Hans Waldmann, who was afterwards deposed and executed, but it illustrates none the less the reform methods of the age. It was not the scattered preachers and chroniclers alone who uttered their Jeremiads on the state of society, but councils and legislatures attempted in their clumsy fashion to stem the drift toward extravagance and immorality.

Even as late as 1519 dancing was forbidden by order of the council. " Let it be announced in the pulpits of the city and written notice sent into the country that since dancing has been forbidden, it is also forbidden to musicians or anyone else to provide dances in courts or other places, whether it be at public weddings or church festivals." · A prohibition of 1500 reads: " In order that God the Lord may protect the harvests which are in the field, and may give us good weather, let no person dance." [17]

Heinrich Bullinger, born in 1504, lived as student, pastor and eventual successor of Zwingli, through the period of the

---

[17] Egli, Akten., No. 82.

Reformation. Between the years 1567 and 1574 he wrote his history of this eventful episode. His description of the condition of the people corroborates the earlier accounts.

"Eighty years ago there was, in the Confederation, in the cities and rural districts, a simple pious, true and upright brave, industrious and frugal people, having the fear of God in their eating, drinking, clothing and household goods, friendly to strangers and pitying the poor. After the treaty with the house of Austria and after the Burgundian wars, as the Confederates began to enter into leagues and agreements with Kings, princes and lords, certain ones of these people began to go to princely courts and entered into the service of Lords and in foreign wars. Upon this followed all sorts of corruption, with intemperance in eating, drinking, foreign clothing and manners, yet this evil did not enter in all at one time but became rooted little by little. For the princes as time went on, began to give this people, not only great pay and rich gifts but also secret pensions and public rewards and gifts. Through this, pride as well as envy and hatred has increased among the Confederates."

"Not long after the Swabian war, when the French were conducting many campaigns in Italy, at Milan and Naples, in the year of the Lord, 1503, the Confederates prohibited all foreign wars and also pensions and gifts from foreign princes and lords. But as the lords did not cease their enticements and, as the prohibition was not maintained it was not long after this time that many were found among the Confederates who had money from three or four lords. In eating and drinking they were not only intemperate but extravagant and princely, taking pride in silver plate and assuming airs with their clothing and silks and satins. In adultery and fornication they were scandalous and altogether unbearable, for at that time there were rivals for the Confederation, the Pope, the Emperor, the French, the Spaniards, the English, Venetians, the Milanese, the Savoyards and other lords had their embassies which they kept continually at the diets of the Confederation and poured out gold over

the Confederates. Such things made the Confederates proud
and spoiled so that they were finally led into a destructive
war with the crown of France on account of Milan. Then
after they had set up the Duke Maximillian in Milan, and
had bound themselves to him and to the Pope, they were
in the year 1515, at Maringano, near Milan, overthrown
and badly beaten by the French. On account of such a
glaring evil, for Zürich in that battle lost about 1500 men,
the rural part of Zürich made a great riot before the city
of Zürich, for they had agreed a long time before to let all
princes and lords alone and to receive no more pensions or
salaries or gifts from any prince or lord whatever. Not
long after, in the year 1517, the Confederation made a peace
with France and from that time on the city and country of
Zürich was in peace and prosperity."

" But the other states ran after princes and lords, and had
many pensioners and there grew up, on this account, more
than before a new nobility in the Confederation, rich in
clothing, extravagant in building, intemperate in eating and
drinking, unendurable in all kinds of arrogance and conducting the government according to their own will with aston-
ishing practices, wherefore the longer it went on the more
division, evils and corruption, as one may easily see in the
history which follows." [17a]

At the same time that the foreign gold was flowing into
the country the economic situation of the Swiss was deterior-

---

[17a] Bullinger points out further the evil effects of the sudden riches
which came into Switzerland. The people, and especially officials,
were made haughty and overbearing by their rapid access of wealth.
He gives an account of the journey of one of the district governors
sent out by Lucerne. On the road the governor and his suite allowed
themselves all sorts of freedom and riotous living. Passing by the
nunnery of Töss they opened up the cells of the nuns and then
marched onward, at Winterthur they threw the jugs and glasses,
silver basins and other things which they had at table, out of the
window into the streets. They did the same thing at Frauenfeldt
where they also demolished the stove saying it was nobody's business; they had enough to pay for it. The governor himself had
slashed breeches and shoes and wore gold rings on his toes, and
there was no end to the vanity and extravagance which they showed.
Against all of this Zwingli protested sharply. Bullinger, Reformation, p. 33.

ating. Agriculture was neglected by the most vigorous part of the population. The soldiers brought back money, but with it corrupt habits and a disinclination to labor in the ordinary pursuits of life. The bribes and pensions received by officials were not likely to be used in industry and the inequalities in the distribution of this ill-gotten wealth were reasons for discontent. Natural sources of gain were neglected in the pursuit of the artificial.[18]

[18] W. Claasen, Schweizer Bauernpolitik im Zeitalter, Ulrich Zwinglis, Chap. I. "Reislaufen und Landwirtschaft."

CHAPTER V.

Morals of the Clergy.

The condition of the clergy just previous to the Reformation is a subject which eludes the investigator who desires the exact truth in statistical form.   Most of our information on this point comes from writers who eventually joined the reform movement, and, writing in the heat of the events, there may have been a tendency to paint in darker colours than necessary.   We may see, however, that the priest was a child of his generation.   Conduct which would not be tolerated at the present time was regarded with indifference at the close of the fifteenth century.   Yet even then there was complaint of ignorance and immorality among the clergy, and we are compelled to admit that there were many individual cases of immoral practices, if we do not go so far as to indict the Church as a whole.

Authentic instances are on record of monks given over to debauchery.   The waste of monastic property was a common complaint, and the city of Zurich had assumed the control or supervision of all endowments of this kind within its territory.   But one cannot assume that the clergy as a whole were lost to all sense of moral decency, nor do we need such facts to account for the Reformation.

The attention of good men was early called to abuses which needed reform.   For instance, Christopher, Bishop of Basel, in 1503 addressed the synod of his diocese on the subject of the immorality of the clergy, and published a body of regulations which were to be enforced with new vigour.   His language is decidedly unequivocal.

" Since we have learned with the greatest chagrin that the greater part of the priests of our city and diocese when they are called to conduct the funeral services of nobles and

other persons, give themselves up to gaming and drunken-
ness, so that many of them at times sit the whole night at
play; others exhaust themselves with swilling and drunken-
ness and sleep the whole night through on the benches, and
by other extraordinary excesses bring scandal, disgrace, and
derision upon the clerical profession: Therefore, we command that all clergymen who are so invited, and all others,
shall not give themselves up to dicing and card-playing, nor
to other irregular and disgraceful actions at any time whatever, and especially in taverns and rooms belonging to the
laity, etc."

A tendency to imitate the world in clothing led to ordinances which forbade the wearing of coloured silks, flowing
sleeves, slashed mantles, or jewelry; nor should they wear
swords, knives, or other weapons, unless travelling. The
public worship should be conducted with fitting decorum.

" The clergy shall see to it that during the worship in the
church they do not walk up and down with laymen or other
clergymen, as we have known it often to happen in certain
collegiate churches of our bishopric, nor shall they go out
upon the market in choir dress during worship to buy eggs,
cheese, or anything else."

Regarding superstitious practices, Bishop Christopher
speaks with words which are as true for all time as for his
day:

" Since experience teaches that certain pilgrimages and
the frequent coming together of the people before certain
pictures, or even at profane places hidden in mountains and
woods, is not so much in consequence of true appearances
as of false dreams, or of the imagination of a sick phantasy,
and the blinding of the senses, and that, in accordance with
their idle and ignorant beginning, a vain and ridiculous result has come from them: Therefore we forbid that in
future the simple folk shall be deceived through their cre-
dulity, or be deceived by invented or superstitious miracle
stories, etc."

Other sound admonitions are included in this pastoral

letter, but only those which acknowledge the presence of gross evils, or immoral tendencies, are here quoted.[19] Bishop Hugo of Constance, in a similar pastoral letter of the year 1517, is grieved to find that many of the clergy are not only given to drinking and gambling, but many are openly living with concubines. He orders them to remove all such suspected women from their houses and to set a bettter example to the laity.[20]

A curious commentary on popular beliefs is the report of the Governor of Baden to the Federal Diet of 1494. He states in a most matter-of-fact way that he has burnt a witch, who left a husband and some property.[21] He desires instructions as to the disposal of these goods. The Diet, as if it were a mere matter of routine, directs him to hold her property for the Confederation and give the man what belongs to him.

Bullinger wrote as follows concerning the clergy previous to the year 1519:

"At one time during these years when all the deacons of the Confederation were assembled together there were found not over three who were well read in the Bible. The others acknowledged that none of them had read even the New Testament, whereby we may understand how it was with the other clergy, with whom the case was still worse. For, among the clergy there was almost no studying, but their exercise was in gaming, in feeding, and in the practice of all luxuries. The more earnest were accused of hypocrisy. Those who studied somewhat devoted themselves to scholastic theology and canon law. The greater part preached out of sermon books, learning by heart sermons written by monks and printed, repeating them to the people without judgment. . . .

"In the churches the mass had become a market and a place for bargaining, in fact, all sacraments and all things

---

[19] Oechsli, ii., 473. Further citations in Appendix II.
[20] Simler, Sammlung alter und neuer Urkunden zur Beleuchtung der Kirchen-Geschichte, Bd. i., 779, Zurich, 1759.
[21] Eidg. Abschiede, iii., 1451.

which one holds holy became venal and corrupt. The singing in parishes and monasteries was for the most part superstitious, and the monasteries had fallen into all sorts of
scandals and idolatries, where no one of them observed so
much as the first of its own rules, not to speak of God's
Word. Every day new altars, endowments, and endless
numbers of idolatrous pilgrimages were established, to the
great pleasure of the clergy, who threw into their bottomless
sack all that the common man as well as the noble possessed.
Whereupon there was great complaint on all sides." [22]

Bullinger's description of the condition of the laity is so
well confirmed by contemporary authorities previously
quoted that one is obliged to give credit to this account of
the state of the Church.

Positions in the Church were regarded as property, and
very naturally, too, since the appointee was obliged to buy
the right of preferment. Pastorates and canonries could
be obtained from the papal court on the payment of a speci-
fied portion of the revenues of the place. Positions were
rated according to a regular tariff, and matters went so far
that candidates bought the right to succeed to a charge
before it was vacant, and these rights became an object of
speculation in the hands of dealers. Such persons were
called courtesans, because they lived by favours received
from the court of Rome. The class included both foreigners
sent thither to occupy livings and native Swiss who were
recipients of papal appointments.

An unconscious revelation of the condition of affairs is
found in the defence of one of these courtesans against the
charges of the Federal Diet. Heinrich Göldli, a Swiss citizen, was a member of the papal guard, and was accused of
dishonesty in his dealings in livings. He refutes the charge
by showing that he had a legal title in every one of his
transactions. A few of his own statements will show how
these things were regarded.

---

[22] Bullinger, Reformationsgeschichte, i., 3.

" It is true I have in time past taken up livings and have requested them of the Pope. I serve the Pope for no other cause, nor have I any other reward or wage from the Pope, neither I nor others of his Holiness' servants, except such livings as happen to fall vacant in the Pope's month, which his Holiness presents to us, every one in his own country. . . . I hope that although I have made contracts or agreements regarding livings which I have lawfully received from his Holiness the Pope for my services over against an evil day, I have had the power and right to do so, so that I may act as I please with mine own and may gain mine own benefit and advantage."

No one ought to charge him with fraudulent dealing, for " I have never in my life surrendered anything from which I have had profit without I have given written evidence and laid myself under written obligation, so that in case it should be disputed by anybody, and I failed to protect him with my title and at my own expense, in the holding of the living, I should be in duty bound to pay back all costs and damages, as well as all that I have received from him."

" In regard to the third article, that I have sold livings in the same way that horses are sold at Zurzach, I have never in all my life sold a living or bought it in this way, for that is simony, and whoever buys and sells livings ought to be deprived of them—but I have, when I have delivered over a living, by permission of his Holiness, demanded and taken the costs to which I have been put, and also have caused a yearly pension to be allowed me out of the living, a thing which is permitted me by the Pope, and concerning which I have my bulls, letters, and seals, for this is a common custom among the clergy."

In reply to the threat of the Diet that he should be forbidden to hold any more livings in Switzerland, Göldli hopes that his legal rights will be respected, that certain appointments will be left for him to live on, and mentions specifically several reservations which have recently cost him large sums, and for which he expects damages and remuneration.

" Furthermore, the Pope has given me the reservation of the provostship of Zurzach, so that when the present provost, Peter Attenhoter, shall die, this provostship shall fall to me. I have also for this the letter and seal, and have paid the annates, as the first fruits are called to the *camera apostolica.*" [23] Göldli declared later that the purchase of this expectation had cost him 350 ducats.

This appeal for justice gives unconsciously the state of opinion and practice in the appointment of the clergy. The authorities were aroused by the extent of the transactions of one man, but public sentiment does not seem to have been greatly offended in general at the purchase of preferment in the Church. Zwingli himself paid over a hundred gulden to this Göldli before he would let him have the living at Glarus, which Göldli claimed in virtue of his papal letter of investiture.

---

[23] Oechsli, Quellenbuch, ii. 504.

CHAPTER VI.

SWITZERLAND AND THE PAPACY.

The relations of the Church in Switzerland to the papacy deserve special attention, for the conditions differed much from the state of things in Germany. For a long time the popes had held the Swiss in high esteem. This was due in general to the doctrinal faithfulness of the mountaineers, and in particular to the devotion with which the Swiss had recently supported the political and military policy of the Papacy. When Julius II. entered into the contest with the other Powers for the possession of Northern Italy he found need for mercenary troops, and applied to the Swiss for aid. Through the persuasions of an energetic Swiss Bishop, Matthias Schinner of Sitten, the confederates came to the help of the Pope with a contingent of men. They were under the impression that it was to be a holy war for the preservation of the Church. When they were undeceived in regard to the objects of the campaign the Swiss were with difficulty persuaded to go into the war, but finally marched into Italy in 1510 and 1512 and performed wonders of valour. The Pope not only paid for these services, but as a token of his pleasure, presented the confederates with a golden sword and a richly embroidered ducal cap, as symbols of their military and political sovereignty, and granted them the title of " Protectors of the Freedom of the Church."

The Swiss came out of these wars with eyes opened to the worldly ambitions of the popes, and their successes were followed by all that train of evils described above under the subject of mercenary service. They gave less heed to the requests of the papacy, and when Leo X. in 1518 asked for twelve thousand men for a crusade against the Turks, the confederates granted only ten thousand, and said if more were needed they would send back two thousand priests to fill up the quota. Although, in fact, these troops were not sent out, as no crusade took place, the reply shows the independent attitude of the Swiss.

In ecclesiastical government Switzerland enjoyed an unusual measure of freedom. The people were accustomed to manage their own affairs and resented interference from the clergy in secular matters. Ever since the fourteenth century they had been gradually limiting the field of ecclesiastical jurisdiction, and the clergy were for the most part subject to the ordinary tribunals. This freedom was not reached without protest, and the struggle was still going on. Disputes with the Church authorities occurred from time to time, particularly in Zurich and Bern. In the latter State the government was in frequent strife with its bishop, and usually got the better of him. At the same time this independence was accompanied with strong respect for the doctrinal authority of the Church and much religious fervour, as may be seen in the many new foundations in honour of the saints, and the abundant pilgrimages. This stands out in curious relief with the loose moral conduct complained of at the end of the century, but the two things are not incompatible.

These friendly relations were strengthened by means common in that age. Like all the other powers the Papacy distributed pensions and gifts to statesmen, politicians, and private citizens. Not all of these could be classed under the head of political corruption, for it frequently occurred that citizens or clergymen were in receipt of small pensions as encouragement in good works or studious pursuits. Documentary evidence of the financial relations of the Swiss to the Popes is found in a report by an agent to the papal treasury for the year 1518. Cardinal Pucci was the almoner of the Pope at this time in Switzerland and his report gives in detail the names of persons and the amounts received.[24]

---

[24] Akten über die diplomatischen Beziehungen der römischen Curie zu der Schweiz, 1512-1552. No. 83, Herausg. von Caspar Wirtz, Quellen zur Schweizergeschichte, Bd. 16, 1895.

Each of the thirteen cantons received 1500 florins in what are called public pensions. Then followed a list of private pensions ranging from 200 down to one florin. In Bern in this class came 1000 florins for the " greater and the lesser Council " because it was not possible to deliver this to individuals. Eleven members of the government including the Schuldheiss (Mayor) the Secretary, and the Treasurer received portions of 70 to 90 florins each, and the Cardinal is confident that they will favour the papal cause. For Zurich there is a detailed account of the state of public opinion and of the prominent persons upon whom he may safely rely. In Zug there are but three large pensions, but there are about 70 persons who receive less than 20 florins a year. The number varies in other cantons but in all of them influential citizens were in receipt of regular pecuniary favors from Rome. The Papacy thus ranged itself alongside the secular states in its diplomatic and military policy and it was but natural that the Swiss people should estimate them all by the same measure. The papal system was not likely to deepen its grasp on the spiritual nature of the people.

In the foregoing circumstances we may also see reasons why Switzerland had never felt the heavy hand of the Inquisition and why the popes were not severe with that people at the beginning of the reform movement. The Papacy was very desirous of keeping on good terms with the Swiss because they were valuable military and political allies.

CHAPTER VII.

EDUCATION.

In depicting the darker side of Swiss society one should not leave the impression that the tendencies of the time were all evil. Reformation was, indeed, imperatively demanded in political and social life, but there were at the same time evidences of intellectual growth which may not be overlooked.

Educational advantages in Switzerland were not as great as in the surrounding countries, but the spirit of the new learning had already taken root. In former times men who were ambitious to pursue wider studies were obliged to go abroad to Paris, Leipzig, Vienna, and other foreign universities, and the Federal Government lightened this task by obtaining advantageous treaty rights for students. In 1460 the University of Basel was opened, founded by the munificence of the learned Pope Pius II., and the Rhine city soon became a centre of enlightenment for an area much larger than Switzerland. This did not prevent scholars from going abroad, but at the same time representative men from all parts of the Confederation were to be found on the list of Basel students, and they met here distinguished lecturers of both native and foreign origin.

Among the Swiss who rose to prominence in the world of scholarship may be mentioned Thomas Wittenbach, who began to teach at Basel, in 1505, as professor of philology and theology. He exerted a great influence upon Zwingli. Heinrich Loriti of Glarus, known to European scholars as " Glareanus," was one of the greatest lights in humanistic studies. After 1513 the great Erasmus made his home in Basel, not for the purpose of teaching, but in order to supervise the printing of his works. He became the centre of a brilliant company of men devoted to the new learning and to the criticism of existing religious institutions. Few of these scholars went over to the reform movement when it came to an absolute break from the Mother Church, but they were tireless in exhibiting the ignorance and abuses found in it.

Nor were their voices confined to a small circle of hearers, for Basel had become one of the great publishing centres of Europe. Printing made its appearance here not long after its discovery, and was so far advanced in 1471 that a strike of typesetters occurred.[25] At the beginning of the sixteenth century the press of Froben was issuing editions of the classics and the works of the Humanists which have themselves become classic in the history of typography. Printing was introduced into various Swiss towns in the last quarter of the fourteenth century, but nowhere attained the celebrity of Basel. In Zurich the press could not have been very important, since the oldest known printing dates from the year 1504. The first substantial publication began under Froschauer in 1521, with translations of Erasmus into the vernacular, and with the issue of the writings of Zwingli. This form of the diffusion of knowledge was, however, appreciated by the educated classes of Switzerland, and as wide use of it was made as the processes of the time would allow.

High schools preparatory to the University were found in a few places previous to the Reformation. At Bern the Humanist who was known as " Johannes à Lapide," returning from a career of teaching in Basel and Paris, opened a school for study of the humanities in the light of the new learning. In this same school taught also Heinrich Wölflin, or " Lupulus," an enthusiastic student of classical antiquity, who had travelled in Italy and Greece, and who was himself a poet of no mean ability. Oswald Myconius at Basel was a teacher of this enlightened order who later transferred his activity to Zurich.

---

[25] " Court Records of Basel," published in *Basler Taschenbuch*, 1863, p. 250, and Oechsli, *Quellenbuch*, ii., 417.

Of primary education not much can be said. Schools were sometimes conducted by the religious houses and cathedral foundations, but a large part of elementary teaching was left to individual enterprise. The lack of text-books made instruction very difficult, but in this respect all countries were alike. Although municipal authorities exercised a supervision over education, public schools had not come into existence. Since teachers depended on their fees for their pay, the rural districts and the smaller towns naturally suffered, and illiteracy was widely prevalent. That private teachers took pupils of all ages for pay may be seen from a schoolmaster's sign which was painted by Holbein in 1516, and which hangs to-day in the Museum of Basel. Freely translated, it reads:

" If there is anyone here who desires to learn to write and read German in the shortest possible time that anybody can conceive of, so that anyone who does not know even a letter beforehand can soon understand, so that he can learn to write down and read his accounts for himself, and whoever is so stupid that he cannot learn, I will teach for nothing and take no reward, whoever they may be, citizen or workingman, women or misses:—whoever desires this, come in here and he will be taught for a reasonable price, the boys and girls by the quarter according to the usual custom."

The pictures which accompany this invitation show a schoolroom in which the master and his wife are teaching small children, with the birch rod ever in hand. On the other side of the sign adults are apparently learning German " in the shortest possible time."

A consideration of this period leads to the conclusion that, while brilliant lights were appearing in the literary world, and a great interest was awakening in the better classes for classical learning and the Scriptures, the facilities for educating the people were very inadequate. There was room for the improvements which were introduced by the Swiss Reformers. Yet the educational movement began before the religious revival and was a cause of the Reformation rather than a result. Myconius, the schoolmaster, and Utinger, the studious canon of the Great Minster, were influential Humanists in Zurich, and helped to bring about the call of Zwingli to that city.

The fine arts flourished in Switzerland, though not to the same degree as in Italy or France. The Renaissance produced several notable artists, of whom Holbein is the greatest. It was the decorative arts, however, which attracted the most attention, for these served the luxury which followed new-gained wealth. From this period date many fine specimens of stained glass, carved furniture, ornamental pottery, and tile-work which do honour to the makers and their patrons. Both public and private buildings show evidences of taste in decoration as well as desire for display.

CHAPTER VIII.

The Cities.

A study of the reform movement in Switzerland shows that the chief centres of agitation were the cities. Furthermore the government of the cities had a deciding voice in the acceptance of changes in the organisation of the Church, and even in changes in doctrine. Hence a word is in place as to the nature of this civic life and the character of the authorities which had such important questions to decide.

At the beginning of the sixteenth century Switzerland contained numerous flourishing towns, but for size and activity they must be measured by the standards of that age. From our point of view city life was contained in very small space. This is due not only to the fact that the population was smaller, but also because of the fortification which was imperative in the Middle Ages. The drawings and engravings of the period represent the towns surrounded with walls and moats. These were still necessary according to the existing methods of warfare, for the larger systems of defence of our day had not yet begun, and any town might consider itself liable to attack at some time. Even if certain places were no longer considered strategic points of importance, nevertheless, their ramparts remained to form a kind of boundary of municipal life. In many of them the walls are standing in part or in whole to-day. At Lucerne one side of the city is still flanked by picturesque towers and battlements, and in many other cities ponderous gateways and fragments of fortifications deep in the interior of the town show the lines of its ancient defence and the former limits of its corporate existence.

These various necessities, as well as the popular taste of that time, obliged people to live in what we should now consider contracted quarters. The streets were narrow and winding. The houses were often large, but their rooms were small and low. The better classes enjoyed a high degree of domestic decoration, but the citizens as a whole appeared to be satisfied with a small measure of light and air. The sanitary condition of houses and streets still lacked enlightened attention, although cities were generally careful to provide good water which the people might get for themselves from the public fountains. Public works were to a considerable degree bounded by the necessity of maintaining the fortifications, even if there had been a demand for greater improvements. Hence the civic life was circumscribed, and one is sometimes tempted to say that the intellectual horizon of the population did not extend much beyond the four walls of their city.

This, however, would be an unfair estimate, and a confusion of intelligence with civic pride. These stone-bound towns manifested the highest degree of local patriotism, and were deeply intent on building up their own material welfare. If this appears at times to be selfish, it is only a part of that individualism which we have already seen in the independence of the States of Switzerland. The cities were the centres of their respective States and their policies.

Bern, Basel, and eventually Geneva became centres of the reform movement, but as the starting point of this current the city of Zurich is the more important to consider. The characteristics of the population, their occupations, and their governments were different in each of these places and all had their influence on the change, but Zurich gave the determining impulses at the start.

The situation of Zurich was favourable to the development of new ideas. Seated at the head of a lake which was on one of the international routes of travel, it had been, all through the Middle Ages, a point which came in contact with the world at large. Its central location in Switzerland brought it early into the growing Confederation, and from the first it was an influential power in its councils. It came to be a frequent meeting-place of the Federal Diet, and as it was also an agreeable city to live in, it became the habitual residence of many ambassadors of foreign Powers. They located there in order to be accessible to the authorities of Zurich and to be within easy reach of the Confederation as a whole.

This imparted to the life in Zurich a certain vivacity which was not found in many other places. The presence of the foreign legations with their retinues of servants gave a stimulus to the trade of the city and to the life of its inhabitants. The taverns and public houses were very numerous. The guild-houses were fine specimens of the architecture of that period, as one may still see in a measure at the present day. There was contact with the outer world, and, consequently, a breadth of ideas which would have been found to so high a degree in no other Swiss town, unless it were Basel. From these facts we may explain two important phenomena in the history of Switzerland. We may see good reasons why Zurich became the pioneer in religious innovation and likewise in political neutrality toward foreign Powers.

The city was a municipal republic, but, although all citizens were given theoretically a voice in its management, it was by no means a democracy, like the alpine cantons. There were two general classes of people: noble and non-noble; of which the latter were naturally the more numerous. All male citizens were, however, classified into guilds according to their occupations. The aristocracy, including both nobility and rich men of affairs, had a special guild of their own, and the trades were grouped in twelve other unions.

The government of the city was vested in a burgomaster and two councils—the Great and the Small. The smaller council contained fifty members, but only one half of them served at a time. In fact there were two burgomasters elected every year, each serving six months at a time, but the vacating burgomaster sat in the councils till the close of the year. The members of the Small Council were all delegates from the guilds except six councilmen at large and the two burgomasters who acted *ex officio*. This may be called the ordinary working administrative council of the city, the twenty-five who acted at any one time not being an excessive number for executive business.[26]

The Great Council was the real legislature of Zurich, since all matters of larger importance were left to its decision. The constitution of this body had been fixed in the revolution of 1489 and remained the same, not only through Zwingli's time, but down to the year 1798. It was also called the Council of Two Hundred, but the exact number was 212. It contained the two parts of the Small Council, eighteen delegates from the " Constaffel," or guild of the aristocracy, and twelve from each of the twelve other guilds. The two burgomasters made up the number.

This Council was the highest source of authority in the State, and was empowered to make laws or even change the constitution without consulting the people. As we have seen, there was no general election of members, but rather a representation of groups, which appears at first sight to be either aristocratic or exclusive. But it should be remembered that the great majority of the men of Zurich were small tradesmen or artisans, and that all of them were included in one or another of the guilds. The leadership in these societies may have fallen at times into the hands of a few men, but, on the whole, this legislature was a fairly representative body. Zurich was a small city, and a council of two hundred members chosen out of a body of voters probably not much exceeding one thousand would give a fair chance for an expression of the popular will.

---

[26] The records of Zurich contain the names of the members of this council from the twelfth century onward. So if desired one might find exactly what men were in office in Zwingli's time, and who helped to bring in the Reformation. In the library of the Johns Hopkins University is a large Folio MS. written sometime after the year 1578, and entitled " Vom ältesten Regiment der Stadt Zürich, so viel man wissen mag." This is a copy of the official register and gives, along with many historical documents, the names of mayors and councilmen " as far back as anyone knows."

These facts are important to observe when changes in the forms of worship take place in Zurich. It was the Great Council which authorized the various reforms. When Zwingli held his famous disputation in 1523, it was in the City Hall and in the presence of the Two Hundred, and they, having been convinced that he was right, passed ordinances to put the new ideas into effect.

The situation is even better understood when one examines into the functions of the Council in detail. Innumerable questions came before it, not only respecting the government of the city, but also in connection with feudal possessions in the canton. These latter involved not only the secular administration, but in nineteen country parishes the right to appoint the parish priest.[27] The Council, therefore, was accustomed to handle ecclesiastical matters in a manner more intimate than merely supervisory.

For many years the government had been requiring strict accounts from the monasteries and convents of the whole territory, and in many cases had appointed managers to oversee their properties. The Council was also accustomed to regulate the private conduct of ministers by punishing evil-doers among them, and occasionally went so far as to order a priest to perform religious functions which he had denied. Zurich was particularly set on restricting the jurisdiction of the clergy, and repeated cases just in this period show that the government did not hesitate to challenge the so-called immunities of the Church.[28]

These facts account for the method pursued by Zwingli, and make the reform movement quite different from that of Luther in one respect. The latter also depended on the civil authorities, but he appealed to the princes of Germany, who were little monarchs in their several provinces. Here

---

[27] Wunderli, Waldmann, p. 157; Appendix, "View of Zurich in 1520."

[28] " Egli, Zürcherische Kirchenpolitik von Waldmann bis Zwingli," Jahrb. für Schweizergeschichte, Bd. xxi.; Remley, "The Relation of State and Church in Zürich, 1519-1523," Leipzig Dissertation, 1895.

it was the people or their representatives who authorized the Reformation. As much might be said of the cities, or of the rural cantons which remained steadfast in the Roman faith—in all cases the people had much to say in the decision.

At this time Zurich contained between 5000 and 7000 inhabitants within its walls, and controlled thirty-five dependent districts outside. Out of the combined population the State could muster about 10,000 men for war. In 1470 there were about 950 households on the tax list of the city proper,[29] and about 52,000 inhabitants in the whole canton. These figures are large only in comparison with other States of Switzerland. Contemporaries considered Zurich the most important of them all.

Within the city a large amount of property was in the hands of ecclesiastics. Besides the cathedral chapter of thirty-four canons there were three parish churches and some twelve chapels. The Benedictine convent, Fraumünster Abbey, had been a retreat for decayed gentlewomen, but was no longer rich nor influential. There were also three convents of mendicant orders and three monasteries of the same class for men.

Of these bodies the cathedral chapter stood in the better relations with the government and the citizens. Some of the canons were scholarly men, others desired at least to be considered such, and the rest of them were influential in one way or another, although not regarded as models of piety. The Augustinians and Capucines were also on good terms with the people, but the Preaching Friars were disliked. They had accumulated a large amount of real estate and houses, and were consequently hated as capitalists and hard taskmasters.[30]

Besides these intramural establishments there were nu-

---

[29] Wunderli, Hans Waldmann, p. 147, Appendix with statistical tables; Bonstetten, Descriptio Helveticæ, in Quellen zur Schw. Gesch., xiii., 254, etc.

[30] In 1467 the clergy all told owned 103 houses in the city, and in 1470 the clerical real estate in the canton was assessed at 82,900 gulden out of a total of 506,500 gulden.

merous monasteries and chapters scattered about the territory of Zurich,[31] all of which would be affected by any change
in the established order of worship. Church-building was
not neglected, for some important restorations date from this
epoch. The picturesque *Wasserkirche* was built up new at
great expense, and the tall, pointed spires which formerly
stood on the cathedral were added during the same period.
Some of the best village churches of the canton were built
about the close of the fifteenth century. Much money was
given for religious foundations, masses, and benevolences,
and much time was spent in local pilgrimages. Shrines on
the Zurichberg, in Leimbach, Altstetten, Küssnacht. and
other places in the vicinity had constant visitors. The
abbey of Einsiedeln was resorted to by hundreds of citizens
and strangers at special seasons, so that the ceremonies of
religion were constantly in view. Yet the social condition of
Zurich was bad. Idleness, luxury, and contentions increased
in spite of laws and magistrates.

In looking over the two or three decades which introduce
the sixteenth century it is seen to be a period of great vital-
ity. Energy, life, movement, have seized the people. They
are conscious that some things are wrong and remedies have
begun to be applied, but this energy itself has been led into
the wrong path. The arts of war appealed to the manly
instinct but brought corruption in their train. The triumphs
of intellect and the conquests of the new learning had at
first great difficulty in making headway, because the Swiss
were for the time pre-occupied with things military and in
the enjoyment of ill-gotten gains. Into this path they had
been enticed, not only by the powers of this world, but by
the apostolic representative of the kingdom of light. No
single State of Switzerland was at first powerful enough to
hinder this decline, and the feeble Federal Government met

---

[31] In 1470 there are 14 on the tax list. In 1520 the number of
foundations is the same. The number of parishes was 103, with
about 150 pastors and numerous chaplains. (Wunderli, Waldmann,
p. 158).

it only with resolutions, which stood a moment unobeyed
and were then repealed. It was logical, therefore, that the
movement which bears the name of Zwingli should begin
with an attack upon political corruption and appeal to the
patriotic sentiment of the free-born Swiss citizen.

APPENDIX I.

THE DIET AND MERCENARY ENLISTMENT.

Protest had been made against this system almost from the beginning of it but at the close of the fifteenth century complaints were more frequent than ever. It became necessary for the central government to express its views. The ordinances passed by the Federal Diet did not accomplish much but they show the drift of public opinion and give evidence of the evil that is complained of. To show the extent and frequency of these ordinances the following additional examples are given, all of them from the *Eidgenössische Abschiede* vol. 3, part 1.

1479, January 14, Lucerne. Every canton should require the soldiers to make oath not to go to war. Some delegates were of the opinion that they should be punished by having their heads cut off.

1479, July 12. Complaint against disobedient soldiers, against their wild life, against their desertion of one army for another without consent of their leaders.

1484, February 2, Lucerne. Complaint against the disorderly conduct of soldiers returned from the war, recommended that all over 14 years should take oath not to enlist in a foreign war without consent of the authorities under pain of confiscation and death. At the same time complaint against scandalous clothing.

1486, December 2, Zürich. Complaint against foreign enlisting officers. Letters from the king of France saying that he had given presents to soldiers who never kept word with him. The territorial governments in various places ordered to capture and imprison all soldiers who have been fighting under the German emperor and to keep them until each has paid five pounds fine and taken oath not to enlist without the permission of the authorities.

1488, June 16 to 24. Baden. Complaint from Appenzell that their soldiery have enlisted in France without permission. They request that the punishment be left to Appenzell, not to the confederation. Question of the disposal of the booty taken from Charles the Bold. Whether twelve thousand pounds should be accepted for the great diamond taken.

1488, December 15. Zürich. The German emperor requests the confederates not to allow their soldiers to enlist in France without permission. Governor of Baden ordered to imprison soldiers returning from France until they can pay ten pounds fine. The bishop of Constance requested to punish soldiers from Baden who ran away to war. Various cities written to that they must punish their disobedient soldiers. St. Gallen and Appenzell state that they are ready to make a mutual ordinance against disobedient soldiers. Zürich requested to write to the king of France that he should dismiss the soldiers of the confederation.

1489, June 18. Baden. Letter from the king of France complaining that he has not been fairly treated in the matter of soldiery. He offers 10,000 francs yearly on condition that the Swiss allow him 3,500 soldiers and for a campaign in upper Burgundy to allow 4,000 to enlist if he requires. Delegates to refer this to their home governments.

1492, June 28. Baden. Complaint against scandalous clothing and the wearing of weapons by soldiers.

1492, August 11. Ordinance of Schwyz recommended against scandalous clothing.

1492, August 28. Ordinance recommended against unauthorized enlistment. Fine of five Gülden and ten days imprisonment on bread and water.

1495, January. Complaint against soldiers from the forest cantons who assist in unauthorized enlistment and act insolently toward the authorities. Recommended that the ringleaders be punished. Names and details given extensively.

1495, March 13. Zürich. Meeting of the five cantons with Freiburg and Solothurn, consideration of the matter last spoken of. The five cantons urged to act in common against these evils.

. 1495, July 9. Every canton to take care that its citizens shall enter no foreign war until date announced by authorities.

1495, July 18. Uri and Schwyz announce that 1200 of their soldiers have run away and enlisted with the duke of Orleans. They say that they could not hinder it and request the confederation to do what it can to stop this evil. Resolution passed that the confederation shall let all foreign lords, kaisers, kings or princes alone and that they will receive from them no more pensions or gifts nor allow any more of their soldiers to enlist under them.

1496, March 7. Lucerne. Consideration of proposals on the part of the king of France that the Swiss should act as mediators between him and the papal government, saying that he has no evil intentions against the latter. He desires to have the confederates enter into a treaty with him.

1496, July 5. The king of France and the duke of Orleans to be written to in regard to the soldiers who were in the battle of Novarra requesting that they should give them their pay and discharge. Every canton requested to punish soldiers enlisting without authority, with a heavy fine. The governors of the federal territory ordered to forbid the same thing.

1496, October 4. The abbot of St. Gallen states that he has endeavored to keep his soldiers from enlisting and has allowed no one to go out under foreign banners, that he stands on the side of the confederation although he is really a citizen of the Roman empire. The abbot is warned that he must take a more definite stand on the side of the confederation. The confederation is warned against persons who are stirring up strife by entangling foreign alliances. Every canton is further warned against enlisting officers who are endeavoring to get soldiers to go into Lombardy under the German Emperor.

1497, April 5.   Reasons given why those who have enlisted without authority, shall take the punishment which is
due them.   Consideration of the way in which pensions from
outside governments shall be treated, declared unwise at
the present moment to turn aside the pension from France
for political reasons therefore the question whether special
or general pensions · shall be refused deferred to another
meeting.

1497, April 16.   The two lords, the king of France and
the emperor of Germany requested to send home the soldiers
who had run away to enlist with them.

1498, August 13.   The soldiers who have enlisted against
the king of France and are now in Burgundy send a request to the confederates that they shall allow no soldiers
from the confederation to come out to fight against them.
An embassy from the emperor of Germany received who endeavors to disentangle complications arising from foreign
enlistment in his armies.

1498, October 22.   Complaint against persons who are
endeavoring to enlist Swiss soldiers for a campaign in
Swabia.   Day set to consider the matter.

1498, November 19.   Question whether the soldiers who
have gone out from the confederate territory shall be punished or not, to be decided at the next meeting.

1499, March 11.   Various rules laid down for the conduct of war including one which declares that every canton
shall make its citizens take oath that when they hereafter
went into battle that they would make no prisoners but kill
all " as our pious ancestors have always been accustomed."

1499, June 23.   Complaint against Bern that she does
not repress foreign enlistment, as well as she might.

1499, December 16.   Certain captains written to that
they shall prevent their soldiers from taking wine or grapes
which belong to the confederation, and since soldiers pay no
attention to the order from their captains they shall be written to directly and threatened with punishment.

APPENDIX II.

1503.

Pastors at the giving of the sacrament shall demand no payments of any kind . . . .

Since it is unfitting that during the public worship the Chorherren and other clergymen whose duty it is to carry on the worship and to think upon psalms and hymns and spiritual songs, that they should talk and carry on conversation disturbing to the worship, therefore, we warn the clergy . . . to sing and to read the canonical hours so that they omit nothing and do not mingle idle conversation with it.

*　　*　　*　　*　　*　　*　　*

The clergy shall see to it during the worship in the church that they do not walk up and down with laymen or other clergy as we have known that it has often happened in certain collegiate churches of our bishopric, nor shall they go out upon the market in Choir dress during worship to buy eggs, cheese or anything else. But on the contrary they shall remain in church during that time and be present in the choir and assist with diligence in the praise of God. · . . .

We command that the clergy of our city and diocese shall wear in the streets and particularly in the churches, long clothing suitable to their profession. Not silk, either red or green, nor such as are lined with party-colored or red silks, nor such as have lined lapels, nor such as are open at the breast, nor such as have a great cord around the neck, nor such as have sleeves too long and too wide. They shall not go about carrying weapons or swords, daggers or long knives except when travelling. . . . . .

Clergymen shall not wear mantles which are open before and slashed, nor such as are closed all around the neck with great cords or closed on one side and open on the other shoulder so that the clothing which is underneath may be seen.

Clergy shall not wear any jackets or wamusses, as they are called among the people, with sleeves which hardly cover the elbow. The collars of the jackets shall be of the right height and shall not be so low that the neck shows bare both before and behind. Nor shall they carry in such collars, pins or rings of silver, or of other metal or material.

 * * * * * * *

Clergy shall wear no rings on their fingers except when the use of them is allowed by their position or the privilege of their rank. The clergy shall wear no improper shoes nor be looking after fashions but they shall wear good and simple kinds without points, trimmings, or strikingly deformed blunt points. They shall be broad on the instep, and shall cover the whole foot and not simply the toes after the manner of the soldiers.

 * * * * * * *

The greater number of the clergy who have canonries who have received the holy orders in our diocese have not been ashamed to let their hair grow too long and have used different artificial means, for example curling with curling irons and changing the color. [Forbidden. Clergy must wear their hair in proper length with tonsure and face shaven.]

The clergy when they celebrate the mass and when they are in cities and castles shall not go about with uncovered legs but shall wear trousers and other leg coverings befitting the clerical profession, in order to cover the nakedness of the legs which is not proper for honorable priests or for decent men in general.

Clergymen on the day of their first mass and at weddings of the laity shall refrain from dancing and idle theatricals and shall not permit in their churches or church yards, dances and games, except representations of God and the

Saints, nor shall they have trading and fairs nor the noise of worldly courts in these places dedicated to God. Clergymen shall refrain from carrying on business or holding auctions in the church but they shall conduct themselves reverently and worthily, remembering that the house of the Lord is the house of prayer, etc. The clergy shall keep no taverns nor become merchants nor carry on trade in business, whereby they buy grain, wine, horses or other things of any kind whatever, at a low price in order to sell dearer. If, however, there are clergy whose incomes are not sufficient they may get themselves a living by the practice of some honorable art as with the writing or binding of books or the writing of music or similar work.

* * * * * * *

The clergy shall not buy or obtain any goods that have been stolen or taken as spoil.

The clergy shall live chastely, temperately and modestly. They shall not have in their houses any women whose life and doings are suspicious of trifling. . . . . .

Experience has taught us that many regular and secular clergy who sow the words of God in our city and diocese, permit themselves sometimes to preach against each other to the perplexing and the making of a bad example for the people. Therefore we forbid that in future any preacher whether he be regular or secular, shall preach in the pulpit against the sayings of another. But, if any of them shall preach errors, heresies or anything against the privileges of another that shall be reported to us or to our vicar so that no disturbance to the people or injury to the soul shall be brought about by public dispute. . . . . .

We command also to all that they sow the word of God, that they preach often and diligently the way that children may be brought up in good manners since it is the most useful to begin the reformation of the church with the children. They shall not speak irreverently and wantonly of their prelates and superiors nor in their preaching in any way despise the prelates of the church, a thing which is already forbidden by the duty of holy obedience, and under threat of the eternal curse. So that the poison of disobedience, the corruption of strife, the biting of scandal, may not proceed out of those who should be diligent in obedience, in edification and in love. The giving of alms, the affair of the poor, of the abandoned, the widow, the orphan and other suffering persons they shall faithfully maintain.[32]

---

[32] Oechsli, Quellenbuch, II, 473, citing Statuta Synodalia Basiliensia, fol. V, sq.; XI sq.; XV sq.

BIBLIOGRAPHY.

Selected references for a study of Switzerland at the beginning of the sixteenth century.

GENERAL AND CONSTITUTIONAL HISTORY.

J. Dierauer: Geschichte der schweizerischen Eidgenossenschaft. 2 vols. 1887, 1892.

K. Dändliker: Geschichte der Schweiz. 3 vols.

—————— History of Switzerland. 1 vol.

A shorter work translated into English.

B. Van Muryden: Histoire de la Nation Suisse. 3 vols. 1896-1899.

J. C. Bluntschli: Geschichte des schweizerischen Bundesrechts von den ersten ewigen Bünden bis auf die Gegenwart. 2 vols. 1849-52. Vol. 1, new edition, 1875.

C. Hilty: Die Bundesverfassungen der schweizerischen Eidgenossenschaft. 1 vol. 1891.

Published at the same time in French as "Les Constitutions Fédérales de la Confédération Suisse."

J. M. Vincent: Government in Switzerland. 1 vol. 1900.

EARLY DOCUMENTS AND CHRONICLES.

Amtliche Sammlung der älteren eidgenössischen abschiede, 1245-1798. 8 vols. 4to. Published by order of the Federal Government under the direction of the Federal Archwist.

Gerold Edlibach: Chronik, 1436-1517. Edited by J. M. Usteri, in Mittheilungen der Antiquarischen Gesellschaft in Zürich, Bd. IV (1846).

Valerius Anshelm: Chronik. Herausgegeben durch E. Bloesch im Auftrag des Historischen Vereins des Kantons Bern. 1884, etc.

Johannes Stumpf, in Zürich. Chronik. Printed first by Froschauer in 1548.

Egli. Aktensammlung zur Geschichte der Züricher Reformation, 1519-1533. Zürich, 1879.

C. Wirz: Akten über die diplomatischen Beziehungen der römischen Curie zu der Schweiz, 1512-1552. Quellen zur Schweizer Geschichte. Bd. 16. 1895.

W. Oechsli: Quellenbuch zur Schweizergeschichte. 2 Bde. 1886-1893.

J. J. Simler: Sammlung alter und neuer Urkunden zur Beleuchtung der Kirchengeschichte vornehmlich des Schweizer-Landes. 2 Bde. 1759-1763.

Heinrich Bullinger: Reformationsgeschichte. 3 Bde. Edited, J. J. Hottinger and H. H. Vögeli, 1838-1840.

MODERN COMMENTATORS ON SPECIAL TOPICS.

J. C. Bluntschli: Staats- und Rechtsgeschichte der Stadt und Landschaft Zürich. Zweite Auflage. Zurich, 1856.

T. Geering: Handel und Industrie der Stadt Basel. 1 Bd. 1886.

S. Vögelin: Das Alte Zürich historisch und antiquarisch. Zweite Auflage. 2 Bde. Zurich, 1878.

Th. von Liebenau: Das Alte Luzern. 1881.

—— —— Gasthof und Wirtshauswesen der Schweiz in älterer Zeit. 1891.

Ch. Kohler: Les Suisses dans les Guerres d'Italie de 1506 a 1512. (Memoires et Documents publiés par la Société d'Histoire et d'Archæologie de Genève. Tom 24, 1897.)

J. Zemp: Die Schweizerichen Bilderchroniken und ihre Architectur-Darstellungen. Zurich, 1897.

W. Claasen: Schweizer Bauernpolitik im Zeitalter Ulrich Zwinglis. (Ergänzungshefte zur Zeitschrift für Social- und Wirthschaftsgeschichte. Berlin, 1899.)

Hans Waldmann: The year 1889 brought forth numerous monographs on the dictator of Zürich and the Revolution of 1499. These all throw light on the social conditions of the period. Among the authors may be cited, K. Dändliker, W. Oechsli, Franz Waldmann, G. Wunderli.